50+ Greatest Classics for Bassoon

Over 50 Favourite Melodies from the world's greatest composers arranged especially for Bassoon starting with the easiest

Amanda Oosthuizen

Jemima Oosthuizen

The Brilliant Bassoon Series
Wild Music Publications
www.wildmusicpublications.com

We hope you enjoy 50+ *Greatest Classics for Bassoon!*

Take a look at other exciting books in the series
Including: *The Brilliant Bassoon book of Christmas Carols, Christmas Duets for Tubas, The Brilliant Bassoon Christmas Bonanza, Moonlight and Roses, Chocolate and Champagne, Easy Tunes from Around the World,* and more solos and duets.

For more information on other amazing books please go to:
http://WildMusicPublications.com

For a **free** sample of our book of **Christmas Carols** AND a **free play-along backing track** visit:

http://WildMusicPublications.com/**secret32-bassoon-track12/**

And use the password: **BSNtrack4U**

Happy Music-Making!

The Wild Music Publications Team

To keep up –to-date with our new releases, why not **follow us on Twitter**

@WMPublications

© Copyright 2016 Wild Music Publications

The music in this book is protected by copyright and may not be reproduced in any way for sale or private use without the consent of the author.

Information

Tempo Markings

Adagio – slow and stately
Adagio lamentoso – slowly and sadly
Alla Marcia – like a march
Allegretto – moderately fast
Allegretto pomposo – fast and pompous
Allegro – fast and bright
Allegro assai – very fast
Allegro grazioso – fast and gracefully
Allegro maestoso – fast and majestically
Allegro vivace – fast and lively
Andante – at walking speed
Andante maestoso – a majestic walk
Andante moderato – a moderately fast
Andante non troppo – Not too fast
Andantino – slightly faster (or sometimes slower) than Andante
Andantino ingueno – not fast but with innocence
Lento - slowly
Maestoso - majestically
Moderato - moderately
Moderato con moto – moderately with movement
Molto allegro – very fast
Molto maestoso – very majestically
Presto – extremely fast
Tempo di mazurka – In the time of a mazurka - lively
Tempo di valse – In the time of a waltz
Vivace – lively and fast
Vivo - lively

Tempo Changes

rall. – *rallentando* – gradually slowing down
rit. – *ritenuto* – slightly slower

 fermata – pause on this note

Dynamic Markings

dim. – *diminuendo* – gradually softer
cresc. – *crescendo* – gradually louder
cresc. poco a poco al fine – gradually louder towards the end

pp – *pianissiomo* – very softly
p – *piano* – softly
mp – *mezzo piano* – moderately soft
mf – *mezzo forte* – moderately loud
f – *forte* – loud
ff – *fortissimo* – very loud

gradually louder
gradually softer

Repeats

D.C. al Coda – return to the beginning and follow signs to Coda ⊕
D.C. al Fine – return to the beginning and play to *Fine*

A repeated passage is to be played with a different ending.

Articulation

staccato – short and detached
sempre staccato – play staccato throughout

accent – played with attack

tenuto – held – pressured accent

marcato – forcefully

Ornaments

trill – rapid movement to the note above and back or from the note above in Mozart and earlier music.

mordent – three rapid notes – the principal note, the note above and the principal.

acciaccatura – a very quick note

appoggiatura – divide the main note equally between the two notes.

Contents

Adagio, Clarinet Concerto – Mozart	24
Allegro, Eine Kleine Nachtmusik - Mozart	14
Anitra's Dance, Peer Gynt – Grieg	25
Ave Maria – Gounod	2
Ave Verum Corpus – Mozart	5
Berceuse, Dolly Suite – Fauré	19
Bridal March, Lohengrin – Wagner	26
Brindisi, La Traviata – Verdi	26
Dance of the Hours, La Gioconda – Ponchielli	12
Dance of the Sugar Plum Fairy – Tchaikovsky	17
Dido's Lament, Dido and Aeneas – H.Purcell	25
Emperor Waltz – J.Strauss	18
Finale, Canirval of the Animals – Saint Saëns	31
Flower Duet, Lakmé - Delibes	27
Galop and Can-Can, Orpheus in the Underworld – Offenbach	23
Grand March, Aida – Verdi	22
Grand Waltz, Opus 18 – Chopin	10
Habanera, Carmen – Bizet	18
Hallelujah Chorus, Messiah – Handel	21
Hornpipe, Water Music – Handel	20
In the Hall of the Mountain King, Peer Gynt – Grieg	29
Jesu Joy of Man's Desiring – J.S.Bach	28
Jupiter, The Planets – Holst	7
La Donne e Mobile, Rigoletto – Verdi	15
Land of Hope and Glory, Pomp and Circumstance – Elgar	6
Lullaby – Brahms	28

March, Nutcracker Suite – Tchaikovsky	17
March, William Tell – Rossini	8
Mazurka, Coppelia – Delibes	19
Morning, Peer Gynt Suite – Grieg	10
Nimrod, Enigma Variations – Elgar	9
Ode to Joy, Symphony 9 – Beethoven	2
O Mio Babbino Caro, Gianni Schicchi – Puccini	24
Pavane Fauré	26
Pizzicato Polka – J.Strauss	15
Polovtsian Dance, Prince Igor – Borodin	4
Queen of the Night Aria, The Magic Flute - Mozart	30
Radetsky March – J.Strauss	22
Ride of the Valkyries, Die Walküre – Wagner	21
Rondo, The Moor's Revenge – Purcell	13
Slavonic Dance 1 - Dvorak	7
Spring, The Four Seasons – Vivaldi	2
Swan Theme, Swan Lake – Tchaikovsky	14
The Blue Danube – J.Strauss	3
The Elephant, Carnival of the Animals – Saint Saëns	3
The Queen of the Night Aria – Mozart	30
The Sorcerer's Apprentice – Dukas	23
The Swan, Carnival of the Animals – Saint Saëns	11
Toreador's Song, Carmen – Bizet	8
Valse Lente, Coppelia – Delibes	13
Voi Che Sapete, Marriage of Figaro – Mozart	9
Waltz, Die Fledermaus – J.Strauss	16
Waltz, Sleeping Beauty – Tchaikovsky	4
Waltz of the Flowers, Nutcracker – Tchaikovsky	16

Ode to Joy
from *Symphony No. 9*

Ludvig van Beethoven
(1770-1827)

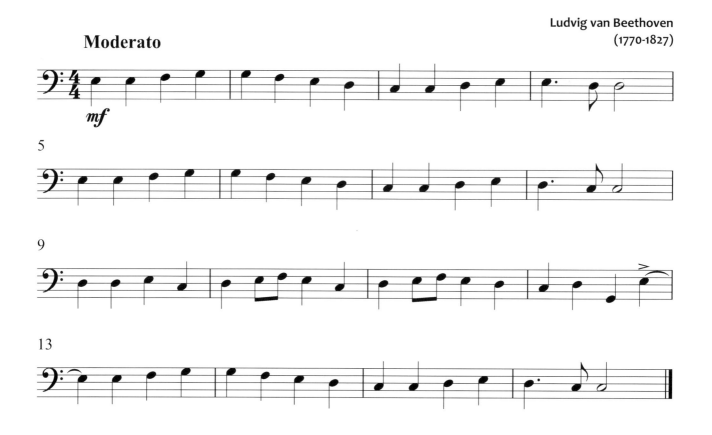

Spring
from *The Four Seasons*

Antonio Vivaldi
(1678-1741)

The Blue Danube

Johann Strauss
(1825-1899)

The Elephant

from *Carnival of the Animals*

Camille Saint-Saëns
(1835-1921)

Waltz
from *Sleeping Beauty*

Pyotr Ilyich Tchaikovsky
(1840-1893)

Polovtsian Dance
from *Prince Igor*

Alexander Borodin
(1833-1887)

Ave Verum Corpus

Wolfgang Amadeus Mozart
(1756-1791)

Land of Hope and Glory
from Pomp and Circumstance

Jupiter
from *The Planets*

Gustav Holst
(1874-1934)

Slavonic Dance No. 1

Antonín Dvořák
(1841-1904)

March
from *William Tell Overture*

Gioacchino Rossini
(1792-1868)

Toreador's Song
from *Carmen*

Georges Bizet
(1838-1875)

Voi Che Sapete
from The Marriage of Figaro

Nimrod
from Enigma Variations

Grand Waltz
Opus 18

Frédéric Chopin
(1810-1849)

Morning
from *Peer Gynt Suite No.1*

Edvard Grieg
(1843-1907)

The Swan
from *Carnival of the Animals*

Camille Saint-Saëns
(1835-1921)

Bridal March
from *Lohengrin*

Richard Wagner
(1813-1883)

Dance of the Hours
from *La Gioconda*

Amilcare Ponchielli
(1834-1886)

Valse Lente
from *Coppelia*

Léo Delibes
(1836-1891)

Rondo
from *The Moor's Revenge*

Henry Purcell
(1659-1695)

Allegro
from *Eine Kleine Nachtmusik*

Wolfgang Amadeus Mozart
(1756-1791)

Swan Theme
from *Swan Lake*

Pyotr Ilyich Tchaikovsky
(1840-1893)

Pizzicato Polka

Johann Strauss
(1825-1899)

La Donna è Mobile

from *Rigoletto*

Giussepe Verdi
(1813-1901)

Waltz
from *Die Fledermaus*

Johann Strauss
(1825-1899)

Waltz of the Flowers
from *The Nutcracker Suite*

Pyotr Ilyich Tchaikovsky
(1840-1893)

March

from *The Nutcracker Suite*

Pyotr Ilyich Tchaikovsky
(1840-1893)

Dance of the Sugar Plum Fairy

from *The Nutcracker Suite*

Pyotr Ilyich Tchaikovsky
(1840-1893)

Habanera
from Carmen

Georges Bizet
(1838-1875)

Emperor Waltz

Johann Strauss
(1825-1899)

Mazurka
from *Coppelia*

Léo Delibes
(1836-1891)

Berceuse
from *Dolly Suite*

Gabriel Fauré
(1845-1924)

Hallelujah Chorus
from *Messiah*

George Frideric Handel
(1685-1759)

Ride of the Valkyries
from *Die Walküre*

Richard Wagner
(1813-1883)

Galop and Can-Can
from *Orpheus in the Underworld*

Jacques Offenbach
(1819-1880)

The Sorcerer's Apprentice

Paul Dukas
(1865-1935)

24

O Mio Babbino Caro
from *Gianni Schicchi*

Giacomo Puccini
(1858-1924)

Adagio
from *Clarinet Concerto*

Wolfgang Amadeus Mozart
(1756-1791)

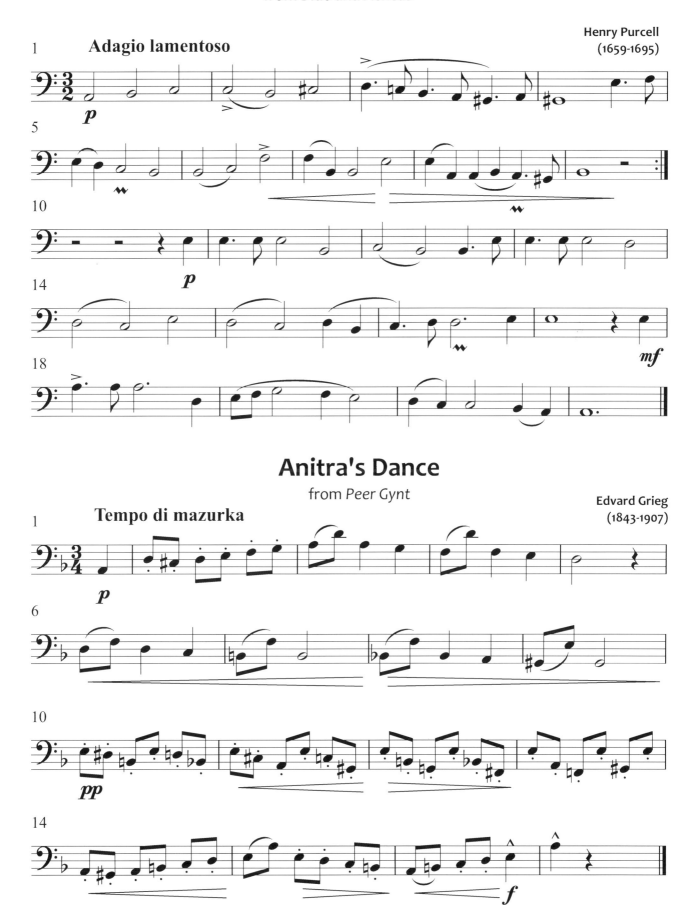

Brindisi

from *La Traviata*

Giuseppe Verdi
(1813-1901)

Pavane

Gabriel Fauré
(1845-1924)

Flower Duet
from *Lakmé*

Léo Delibes
(1836-1891)

Jesu, Joy of Man's Desiring

Johann Sebastian Bach
(1685-1750)

In the Hall of the Mountain King
from *Peer Gynt*

Edvard Grieg
(1843-1907)

The Queen of the Night Aria

from *The Magic Flute*

Wolfgang Amadeus Mozart
(1756-1791)

Finale

from *Carnival of the Animals*

Camille Saint-Saëns
(1835-1921)

If you have enjoyed **50+ Greatest Classics for Bassoon,** why not try the other books in the **Brilliant Bassoon** series!

For more info, please visit: **WildMusicPublications.com**

All of our books are available to download, or you can order from Amazon.

Introducing some of our favourites:

Fish 'n' Ships

Bassoon Music Practice Notebook

Christmas Carols

Trick or Treat – A Halloween Suite

Bassoon Music Theory Book 1

Moonlight and Roses

Very Easy Christmas Duets for Teacher and Pupil

Christmas Duets

Christmas Crackers

Made in the USA
Columbia, SC
12 November 2021

48693734R00022